ANIMAL FAMILIES

Lions

General Editor
Tim Harris

BROWN BEAR BOOKS

Published by Brown Bear Books Ltd

4877 N. Circulo Bujia
Tucson, AZ 85718
USA

and

First Floor
9-17 St. Albans Place
London N1 0NX

© 2012 Brown Bear Books Ltd

ISBN: 978-1-78121-004-8

Managing Editor: Tim Harris
Designer: Lynne Lennon
Picture Manager: Sophie Mortimer
Art Director: Jeni Child
Production Director: Alastair Gourlay
Editorial Director: Lindsey Lowe
Children's Publisher: Anne O'Daly

Library of Congress Cataloging-in-Publication Data available upon request

Publisher's note to educators and parents: Our editors have carefully reviewed the websites that appear on p. 31 to ensure that they are suitable for students. Many websites change frequently, however, and we cannot guarantee that a site's future contents will continue to meet our high standards of quality and educational value. Be advised that students should be closely supervised whenever they access the Internet.

Manufactured in the United States of America

Contents

Introduction

Lions are known for being brave and powerful. Armed with huge dagger teeth and slashing claws, lions are built to hunt.

What makes lions extra special is the way they live. They are not solitary prowlers, like tigers and other wild cats. Lions live in family groups called prides. Lions rear their cubs together, feed together, and hunt together. When a group of lions hunts as a team, it can catch almost anything.

We are going to look at how these lion families spend their lives. This book will tell you how they get on with

⬡ **With its flowing reddish-brown mane, an adult male lion is an unmistakable sight.**

🔊 **A lioness and some cubs. Lionesses give birth to two or three cubs, so some must belong to another mom.**

each other, deal with neighbors, hunt their prey, and bring up their babies. We will see exactly what it is that makes these big cats so special, and just why they are admired and feared.

The king of beasts

The majestic lion certainly deserves its title of "king of the beasts." The other big cats dare not cross it, for a lion will kill a lone leopard if it gets the chance.

   The only real threat to the lion's authority is the burly spotted hyena, which hunts in big packs and has massive, bone-cracking jaws. Hyenas often steal lion kills, but then lions also steal hyena kills.

Lazy lions

Pound for pound, meat contains much more energy than plants. While their grass-eating victims have to spend most of their lives eating, lions need to hunt for just three or four hours a day. This means they can spend most of their time lazing around—and that's exactly what they do.

A lion pride

Some lions live alone, like other cats, but these lone lions are the unlucky ones. Lions prefer to live in a group, or pride.

A lion pride is a big family of up to 12 related lionesses (female lions) and their young, plus up to six adult males. The females do nearly all the hunting and work together to look after their cubs. Lionesses may stay in the same pride for life, but the males are driven out by stronger rival males after

⬇ **A pride of lions rests after eating a meal.**

Two male lions share a meal. Their manes are short, so they are young animals.

Bands of brothers

Young female lions usually stay with their mothers in the pride, but the young males always leave home. Sometimes they wander off alone, but usually brothers and half-brothers leave in small groups. Gangs survive better than loners, so unrelated lone males often form gangs of their own.

two to four years. These takeovers can be violent, and the job of the males is to defend the pride against them.

Lions' territories

Each pride has its own hunting area, or territory. The pride is usually scattered all over it in small groups. If food is scarce, the lions have to roam over a vast area to get enough to eat. Smaller, richer territories are less tiring and easier to defend. The pride's territory is never any bigger than it needs to be. Some lions, usually older males, live alone.

Rivals and allies

Like all animals that live together, lions pass messages to each other. They use sound, touch, scent, and facial expressions to do this.

The most impressive sound made by a lion is its roar, but it can also grunt, growl, snarl, hiss, meow, and even purr like a pet cat. By changing the tone and loudness of all these sounds, a lion can signal different feelings, from happiness to a deadly threat.

Lions back up these sounds by nuzzling, rubbing, and licking. They rub their heads in greeting and often lie close together to keep each other warm and for protection.

Lionesses show affection by licking each other.

The lion's roar

The full-throated roar of a lion is a terrifying sound and can be heard for miles around. Lions often roar to show other lions who's who. A male lion defending his territory, for example, roars to warn off another lion from outside the territory. He may also roar at a rival during an argument, hoping to scare off the other lion without needing to fight.

➲ A lion's roar can be heard far away. It is a warning, telling other male lions to stay away.

Lions have surprisingly expressive faces. They can move their lips and face muscles far more than most animals. They have at least 17 different facial expressions. For a lion that is really useful because it can check its neighbor's mood before doing anything that might annoy it. Annoying a lion is a serious mistake, even for another lion!

Scent signals

Lions use scent signals like tomcats, marking their territory with strong-smelling urine and sniffing any scent marks left by other lions. Lions that are just passing through a territory find this handy because they can keep away from the residents!

Hunting lions

When a lion hunts alone, it may pounce on anything that moves, even rats and birds. Lions are more likely to catch prey if they hunt in a group.

When lions hunt together, they usually target large game animals such as wildebeest, buffalo, and zebra. They have a problem, though. A lion can sprint at 36 mph (58km/h), but an antelope or zebra can streak away at up to 50 mph (80km/h). The only way a lion can catch its fast-moving prey is by creeping close enough—unseen—to spring an ambush.

Dead meat

Lions are expert hunters, but they are scavengers too. They often steal prey killed by hyenas, cheetahs, and leopards. One survey in the Ngorongoro Crater, Tanzania, found that eight out of ten lion "kills" were actually killed by hyenas.

➜ A lioness grabs hold of a wildebeest with its great claws. Next, it will bite its victim's neck to suffocate it.

A lioness chases a warthog through long grass.
Two other lionesses look on, ready to share the kill.

When a pride of lionesses hunts together, it fans out and circles around the prey to cut off its escape. Lions usually hunt at night, but if there is enough long grass to hide in they will hunt in daylight. When the lions have crept close enough to their quarry, they strike. Charging at full tilt, they try to knock their victim to the ground.

Muscling in on a kill

One lion sinks its claws into the animal's back and drags it to the ground. It sinks its huge teeth into the victim's throat to cut off the air supply. The victim soon suffocates, and the lions gather to share the kill. The lionesses do most of the hunting. When it comes to feeding, though, a male often pushes the smaller lionesses aside to grab most of the kill.

Time to mate

Lions can breed all year round. The lionesses are only interested in mating for two to four days every month or so, though.

Sometimes the lionesses go for months without coming into breeding condition, which is called estrus. Then all the lionesses in the pride are ready to mate at the same time.

The males within the pride have to be ready to mate whenever the females are ready, and they have to make sure that trespassing males do not mate with the females first. The males within the pride rarely fight over females because they need each other to help defend the pride against intruders. Males settle the problem by "claiming" females as they become receptive and guarding them through the mating period.

Male guards

Each male can only guard one female at a time. Another male may mate with the female the next

A male lion can tell if a female is ready to mate by her scent. He opens his mouth and wrinkles his nose to detect her scent.

A male lion approaches a female who is ready to mate. She will not always welcome him!

time she comes into estrus. As a result, all the pride males usually end up as joint fathers of all the cubs born that season.

Some lion cubs are fathered by strangers who sneak in and mate with females while the pride males are busy elsewhere. If the outsider lions manage this without being spotted by the pride males, their cubs are raised as part of the pride.

Blood brothers

Lionesses in a pride often come into breeding condition at the same time. That means a lot of cubs are born at once. Male lions are more likely to succeed in life if they have brothers and cousins of the same age. They can leave the pride together in a big group and produce their own cubs.

Lion cubs

A lioness carries her babies inside her for 14 to 15 weeks. She gives birth to two or three cubs, which weigh between 2 and 4 pounds (0.9 to 1.8kg).

The mother goes to a quiet place to have her cubs and hides them carefully before joining the other lionesses to hunt. She returns to feed the cubs on her milk.
 The cubs are born blind and helpless. Their eyes open when they are between three and eleven days old. The cubs start to walk after about two weeks. They stay hidden, though, and always slip out of sight at the slightest alarm. It may be another month or more before they are

Two lionesses with their cubs on an African grassland. Lionesses in the same pride will help look after each others' cubs.

Spotty cubs

Adult lions are tawny yellow; but when they are born, the cubs are covered with dark spots. These markings help protect them from enemies by acting as camouflage in the dappled shade of their hiding places. The spots start to fade at the age of three months and then usually disappear altogether.

Two cubs play. The spots on their fur are beginning to fade.

ready to join the rest of the pride. The lionesses in the pride help look after each others' cubs and even feed them on their milk.

Gradually the young lions learn to take solid food. By the age of three months they are playing at stalking their own prey.

Dangerous days

Playing is not the real thing, though. When they join the pride on a serious hunt, the youngsters often scare off the prey by treating the whole thing as a game. The cubs start to take part in hunts when they are about 11 months old. After about 18 months the young lions are ready to look out for themselves.

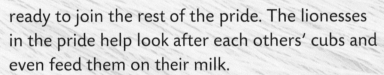

Fighting males

Young male lions are forced to leave the pride by the adult males when they are two years old. If they are lucky, three or four leave together.

Lone male lions have a struggle to survive and often team up with other males. The bigger the gang, the better their chances. The male lions wander for two or three years, often following herds of antelope and zebra. They are big, strong, and fit at the age of five. If they run into a pride defended by older, weaker males, they will attack it.

Winner takes all

The fights can be savage, and losers are sometimes killed. The young males may

This is a young male. He has a short mane but it is not yet fully grown.

Two young males test each other's strength. Real fights are more violent than this.

be beaten back; but if they win, they drive out the pride males, who then become wanderers themselves. The victors take over their territory, the pride lionesses, and their cubs.

Murdering males

For a male lion the most important thing in life is fathering cubs. If a new male takes over a pride, he wants the lionesses to raise *his* cubs, not the cubs fathered by the males he has just defeated. So he kills the cubs.

Sometimes the lionesses defend their cubs by joining forces and attacking the murdering males. This is very dangerous, though, and usually the lionesses have to put up with the situation.

Keeping control

A strong band of male lions may keep control of a pride for four years or more, but a group of two or three is lucky to last two years. This is just long enough to raise one generation of cubs. If the males are driven out any earlier, they could lose all their cubs to the next gang of males. All the effort of breeding will have been wasted. For both males and females it pays to be part of a strong pride.

Lionesses

Lion society is centered on the females. The pride is really a family group of related lionesses: grandmothers, mothers, and daughters.

The pride lives together for many generations. A young lioness has a much safer life than her brothers. She normally stays in the pride with her mother, sisters, and female cousins. Since all the cubs are brought up together, there is no real pecking order, although some individuals are first in line at kills. The lions in a pride look after each other. A young lioness learns to do the same.

When she gets old enough, she joins the other lionesses on hunting trips. It can be risky work, especially if they are hunting big animals like zebra.

⬇ **There is safety in numbers for lionesses.**

Long-lived lionesses

It is a lot less dangerous than fighting other lions, though. This is one reason why there are always more adult females than males. Female lions live longer than males. They can live to be 18 years old. Males usually live to 12 years if they have not been killed in a fight before then.

A lioness begins breeding at the age of four. By this time her father has usually been driven from the pride by a male takeover, and one of the new pride males becomes the father of her cubs. A female lion can give birth to a new litter every 18 to 26 months. She may have five litters before she is too old to breed.

A group of lionesses and their cubs take a welcome drink at a water hole.

Thrown out

If a pride grows too big for its territory, some of the young lionesses may have to leave. They wander like young males, and like them they stand a better chance of surviving if they travel in company. Many die young, but others are accepted into other prides.

Built to kill

A lion is a powerhouse killer. It has both the power and the weapons to hunt large prey. Even hunting alone, it can kill animals four times its own weight.

For one thing, a lion weighs a lot. A male can weigh anything up to 530 pounds (240kg). Even a sleek lioness usually weighs more than 300 pounds (136kg). When a lion leaps on its target, the collision can send the victim sprawling. The only disadvantage is that a lion's weight slows it down when it runs.

The lion uses its teeth to finish off its prey. Like other hunters, it is armed with long, pointed canine teeth, but

A male lion jumps on the back of a wildebeest. The lion will use its strength and weight to pull its victim down.

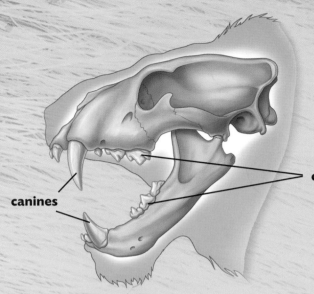

A lion's skull, showing its teeth. The sharp canine teeth at the front act like daggers to kill prey. The scissorlike carnassials in the cheeks shear through the flesh.

canines

carnassials

its jaws are shorter than most. Its jaw muscles can squeeze the teeth together with immense force.

When it has made its kill, the lion can start slicing up the body with its bladelike cheek teeth (carnassials). They are just right for shearing through skin and flesh like scissors. When most of the meat is gone, the lion uses its rough tongue to scrape the bones clean.

Eyes and ears

A hunting lion relies on its eyes and ears. It can even see well by starlight. Sound is less important than sight. The lion can usually see its prey, so it does not need to locate it by sound. It still uses its ears a lot, though, especially at night.

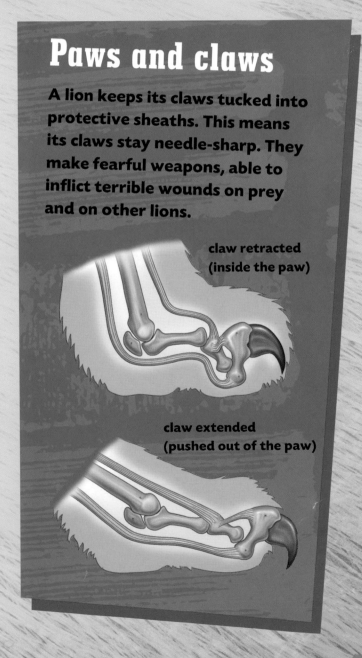

Paws and claws

A lion keeps its claws tucked into protective sheaths. This means its claws stay needle-sharp. They make fearful weapons, able to inflict terrible wounds on prey and on other lions.

claw retracted (inside the paw)

claw extended (pushed out of the paw)

What's in a mane?

Most male and female cats look similar, but with lions the difference is obvious. An adult male lion is a hairy giant with a magnificent flowing mane.

There are other differences, too. A male may weight up to half as much again as a female. In some ways the male's extra weight is a problem. He is less agile than a lioness and cannot run as fast. His big mane may look impressive, but it makes him easier to spot when he is creeping up on prey. So he is not as good at stalking

⬇ **The lioness is strong and sleek. Muscular hindquarters provide power for sprinting, and strong forelimbs can bring down prey.**

and catching prey. Pride males usually leave the hunting to the lionesses.

Why are males so big? A small male would stand no chance against rivals trying to take over the pride. The biggest, strongest males always win. Since the winners father all the cubs, the next generation of males is usually big and strong, too.

🔽 **An fully grown male lion weighs around 416 pounds (189kg). His sister is about 277 pounds (126kg).**

🔼 **As well as making the lion look bigger, the flowing mane protects his neck during fights with other lions.**

The lion's mane

The male's mane starts to grow when a lion is about two years old. It looks magnificent, and it is meant to. Males spend a lot of time trying to scare rival males off their territory, preferably without a fight. So the bigger and meaner they look, the better.

Big cat relatives

The lion is a type of mammal called a carnivoran. This group of animals includes the cats, dogs, weasels, bears, raccoons, civets, and hyenas.

Almost all of these animals eat meat, and many are fierce hunters. Some eat other things as well. And a few, such as the giant panda, are almost totally vegetarian. One feature that most of them share is scissorlike cheek teeth called carnassials. Most carnivorans use these teeth to slice through meat. Cats, which eat almost nothing but meat, have the biggest and sharpest carnassials.

Dogs and bears

Dogs and bears have chewing teeth behind the carnassials, but cats do not have chewing teeth. A cat has a shorter muzzle than a dog or a bear and a more powerful killing bite.

⬅ **The Siberian tiger is the biggest of the big cats. This very rare animal lives in northern China and Russia.**

Cheetahs live on the plains of Africa. They use sheer speed to catch their prey.

Meet the family

There are big cats and small cats. All are built much the same, but they hunt in different ways. Cheetahs, for example, chase their prey very fast. Margays in South America hunt up in trees. Most of the other cats are stealth killers that ambush their victims. Lions are the only cats that hunt in groups.

Tigers

Only one cat is more powerful than a male lion—the tiger. A male Siberian tiger can weigh up to 750 pounds (360kg).

It is a formidable killer and can bring down big prey without the help of a pride. That is partly because it lives in forests, where there is plenty of cover to hide in. A hunting tiger can creep up close to its victim and pounce before it has a chance to escape. The tiger then gets to eat the whole of the kill itself.

Where lions live

African lions are open-country cats. They hunt grazing animals, and to do so they must follow the herds of antelope and zebras across the grasslands.

The open landscape makes life difficult for hunters that stalk their prey because there are few places to hide. Lions get around this problem by hunting in groups. This allows them to survive in some of the most open landscapes in Africa. These include the parched savannas of the Serengeti in the east and the Kalahari Desert in the south.

On these dry, grassy plains lions often have to wander across huge areas to find enough prey. Hunting is easier where there is some cover. Ideal lion country is lush grassland with plenty of scrub and some shady trees.

⬆ The only place where Asiatic lions live in the wild is the Gir Forest in India.

Asiatic lions in India

The only wild lions surviving outside Africa today live in the Gir Forest of northwest India. There are only about 400 of them, living in a wildlife sanctuary that covers 540 square miles (1,400 sq km) of grassland and forest. Since they can ambush prey from forest cover, like tigers do, group-hunting tactics are not so important. Prides are smaller than those of the African lion, with two males and three or four females. They are now protected by law.

Shrinking horizons

Lions were once widespread through much of Africa, southern Asia, and southern Europe. They roamed the deserts of West Asia only 100 years ago. Today there are few lions in India, and they are even disappearing from Africa. Over the last 100 years about half of Africa's lions have been hunted and killed. Many of the ones that are left cannot find enough to eat.

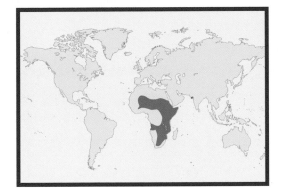

⊕ Areas in the world where African and Asian lions live.

⊕ A pride of African lions relaxes in the sunshine near the Ngorongoro Crater in Tanzania.

Circuses and safaris

The ancient Romans used lions from Africa for their wild beast shows. As part of the show, criminals were thrown to the lions to be killed or eaten.

These grisly events took place in arenas the Romans called circuses. As time went on, circuses became less violent, but lions were still a big attraction.

Lion-tamers trained lions to perform tricks, and between shows the animals lived in cramped cages. Meanwhile, other lions were displayed in zoos, also in small cages. Even if they were well cared for—and many were not—it was nothing like their life in the wild.

➲ **This African lioness is in a zoo. Most modern zoos allow their large animals more space to run around than was once the case.**

Vacationers on a safari jeep watch and photograph a male lion in a Kenyan national park.

"Maneaters"

Wild lions often attack farm animals, especially where their normal prey is scarce. However, maneating lions are rare. This seems strange because people are easy targets. People are slow, easy to stalk, and no trouble to kill. The few lions that regularly kill people are usually too old and feeble to kill anything else.

Zoos and national parks

Today, most lions in zoos are kept in large enclosures where they have grass, trees, and space. In some North American zoos lions are bred in captivity in case they die out in the wild.

Many wild lions live in African wildlife reserves and national parks. There, they are protected from hunters who might want to kill them for "sport." Reserves include the Serengeti National Park in Tanzania and the Kalahari Gemsbok National Park in South Africa. These parks cover vast areas of grassland and forest, allowing their resident lions to live wild and free.

Glossary

camouflage The markings or colors on an animal that make it more difficult for other animals to see.

carnassial A very sharp, bladelike tooth used for cutting meat.

carnivoran A large group of meat-eating animals that includes cats, dogs, bears, weasels, and lions.

cub A baby or young lion.

estrus The state when a lioness can become pregnant.

habitat The kind of place where a particular animal lives.

lioness A female lion.

mammal A kind of animal that is warm-blooded and has a backbone. Most are covered with fur. Female mammals have glands that produce milk to feed their young.

mane The long fur that grows around the neck of an adult male lion.

mate When a male and female get together to produce young.

muzzle An animal's jaws and nose.

pride A family group of lions.

range The parts of the world in which a particular type of animal lives.

retracted When a lion's claws are drawn back into its paws.

savanna Open grasslands with scattered bushes and trees.

territory The area over which a pride of lions ranges.

tropical Having to do with or found within the tropics. These are the hot areas to the north and south of the equator.

Further Reading

Books

Big Cats. S. L. Hamilton. Edina, MD: ABDO, 2010.

Big Cats. Bruce Johnston. San Anselmo, CA: Treasure Bay, 2010.

Big Cats: In Search of Lions, Leopards, Cheetahs, and Tigers. Steve Bloom. New York: Thames and Hudson, 2012.

Everything Big Cats. Elizabeth Carney. Washington D.C.: National Geographic, 2011.

Lions. Amy-Jane Beer. Danbury, CT: Grolier, 2009.

Lions. Aaron Frisch. Mankato, MN: Creative, 2007.

Lions. Tammy Gagne. Mankato, MN: Capstone, 2012.

Lions. Sophie Lockwood. Mankato, MN: Child's World, 2008.

Lions in Danger. Helen Orme. New York: Bearport, 2007.

Websites

African Wildlife Foundation
Lots of information about conservation projects for lions and other African animals.
www.awf.org

BBC Nature
Information about lions' lifestyles with beautiful photographs and clips from TV programs.
www.bbc.co.uk/nature/life/Lion

Lion Research Center
University of Minnesota website with features on lions' daily life, foraging, mating, and social behavior.
www.lionresearch.org

Index